A car has over 14,000 pieces

Trunk

Sedan

Tailpipe

Tailgate

Hatchback

Gas tank door

Radiator grill

Types of

Convertibles have tops that fold back.

Station wagons have a large space in the back for luggage

Sedan cars have two or four doors and a boot.

Hatchbacks have a door at the back that opens upwards.

3

At the controls

Cars are complicated machines but the controls to drive them are quite simple.

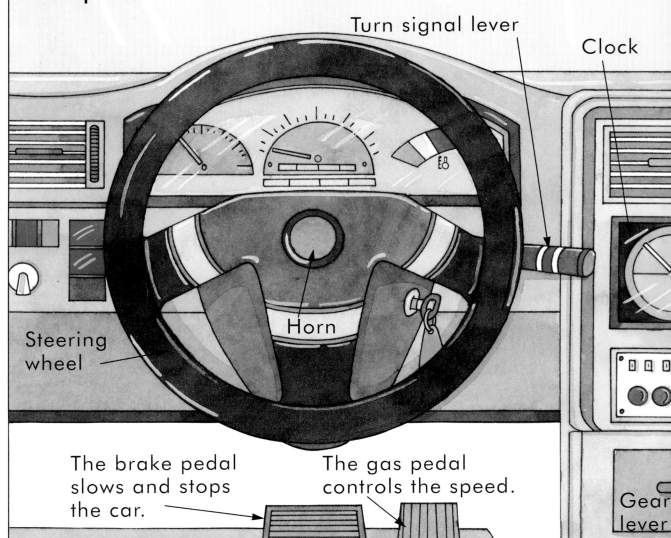

Turn signal lever

Clock

Steering wheel

Horn

The brake pedal slows and stops the car.

The gas pedal controls the speed.

Gear lever

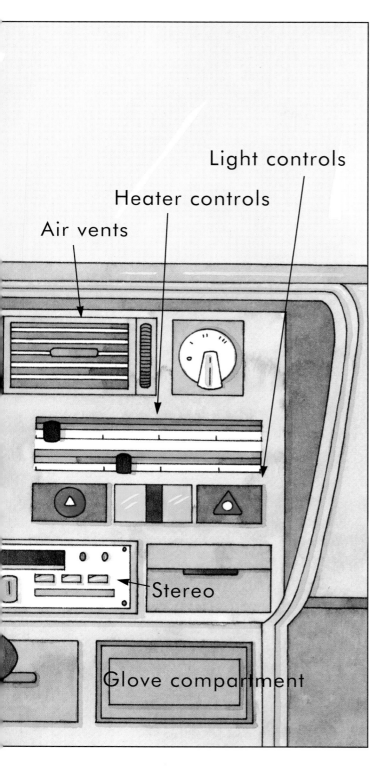

Light controls

Heater controls

Air vents

Stereo

Glove compartment

Control panel

The dials and lights on the control panel give the driver important information.

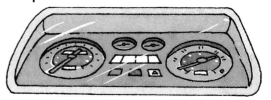

The **low level gas warning light** comes on when the car needs more petrol.

The **temperature dial** warns when the engine is overheating.

The **speedometer** shows how fast the car is going.

Fast, faster, fastest

Sports cars have powerful engines and streamlined shapes so that air can pass over them easily.

Turbo engine

Streamlined shape

Spoiler

Fun Fact

Speeding racing cars go so fast that sometimes they almost take off! Spoilers attached to the car act like upside-down wings, keeping the tires on the ground.

Formula One racing cars are built for one thing—to win races! There is just enough room inside for the one driver.

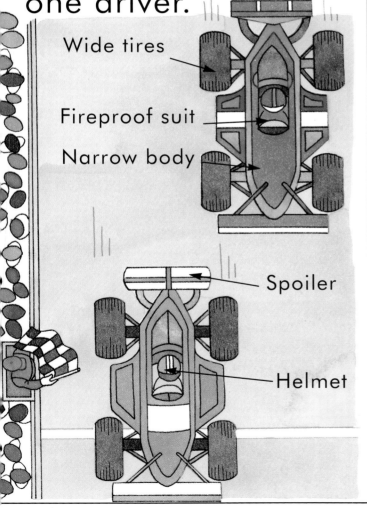

Wide tires

Fireproof suit

Narrow body

Spoiler

Helmet

Built for speed

Slicks Smooth wide tyres called slicks give racing cars extra speed.

Light bodies Racing cars have bodies made of extra-light material.

Powerful engines and lots of gears drive racing cars at speeds up to 250 mph.

Hot rods and rally cars

Hot rods and dragsters are sprinters. They run in drag races. The winner is the fastest to the finishing line— only 1/4 of a mile away from the start!

Spoiler

Cage to protect the driver.

Dragster

Drag strip

Slick-tread tires

Rally cars are long-distance racers. They run in races that last for days, weeks, or even months.

Dragsters go so fast that they need **parachutes** to help slow them down.

Rally drivers have a **navigator** in the car to tell them which way to go.

Fun Fact
The longest rally race ever run was from England to Australia, crossing 19,329 miles.

Tough cars for rough places

Tough cars, called off-road vehicles, are built to bump over rocky ground and splash through water. They can go up steep hills and keep a tight grip on downhill slopes.

On the farm

Outdoor pursuits

On safari

Special features

Ground clearance

The bottom of the car is high to clear rocks and bumps.

Tire tread

Deep tire patterns, called tread, grip slippery or sandy ground.

Four-wheel drive

All four wheels are powered by the engine. If any of the wheels gets stuck, the other wheels can still work.

11

To the rescue

Police cars, fire engines, and ambulances are fitted with special equipment to deal with emergencies. Sometimes they all work together.

Fire Engine

Radio

Hose

Police car

Fun Fact

FIRE, POLICE and AMBULANCE are sometimes written like this so that drivers can read them through their rearview mirrors.

Ambulance

Stretcher

Doing their jobs

Emergency vehicles use blue **flashing lights** and loud **sirens** to warn other drivers to pull over so they can get past.

An **aerial ladder platform** can rescue people from the top of buildings, down cliffs, and under bridges.

Ambulances have **medical equipment** inside to give patients treatment on the way to hospital.

13

Trucks

Trucks carry and deliver loads all over the country and abroad. They have different shaped bodies for the loads they carry.

Outside mirrors set wide for extra vision.

Box body
A moving van carries furniture in its box body.

Curtain-sider
The curtains keep the load dry and in place.

Clips

Drop-sider
The sides of this truck can be dropped down to unload the scaffolding.

Roll-up door

Flatbed body
It is easy to reach
the load once the
sheeting and
ropes are untied.

Truck parts

Straight trucks have
two sets of wheels.
Sometimes the back
wheels are
in pairs.

Chassis The chassis
is the frame of the
truck.

Axle Each set of
wheels is on an axle.

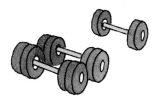

Semis

Semis or two-piece rigs have two parts—the tractor at the front and the semitrailer at the back. Tractors can drive without a semitrailer, but semitrailers cannot move without a tractor.

Wind deflector

Horns

Semitrailer

Airhoses

Engine

Lights

Cab tilt The cab can be tilted for the driver to check the engine.

Night cab Long distance drivers sleep in a night cab.

Cab

Tractor

Airhoses are plastic pipes that carry air for the brakes in the trailer.

Loading and unloading

Different loads need special trucks to move them.

A loading machine fills the dump truck with buckets of earth.

Some trucks are fitted with cranes for lifting their heavy loads.

A forklift truck can load boxes right into the top of another truck.

The middle and top platforms of a car transporter tip to make ramps for driving cars on and off.

On and off

Crane The crane can lift, swing round and lower its head.

Forks Forklift trucks have a two-pronged fork which slots into special wooden loading pallets.

Tipper A rod behind the driver's cab opens like a telescope to tip the truck up.

Tankers

Tankers carry liquid loads
such as gasoline, chemicals,
and milk. They can also
carry powder and granules.

Dairy truck

Gasoline tanker

Gasoline is pumped from the
gasoline tanker into tanks
near the pumps of the
gas station.

Weighbridge

Gauge

Delivery
pipe

Underground storage tank

Milk tankers
Milk tankers collect milk from farms and deliver it to the dairy.

Silo

Pump island

Loads
Dry loads Tankers can tip up to empty dry loads.

Liquid loads are delivered through a pipe.

Dangerous loads have warning stickers. In an accident, a code tells the rescue workers what is in the tanker.

Trucks for special jobs

Some trucks are fitted with machinery for doing special jobs.

Road sweeper
A brush whirls round cleaning and sweeping.

A giant vacuum pipe sucks up the dirt and leaves.

Snow plow

Strong headlights are needed to work in blizzards.

A spreader swirls salt and grit onto the road to stop it icing up again.

A blade scrapes and pushes snow and ice off the road.

Garbage truck

The back section lifts up and the garbage is tipped out at a dump site.

Rotating blades crunch up the garbage.

Garbage cans are emptied into the truck.

Ultra-heavy hauler

These trucks carry enormous loads. An extra truck is often needed to push from behind or to pull from the front.

A **police escort** with flashing lights and sirens travel with the load to warn other drivers.

Index

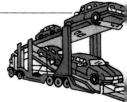

Ambulances **12-13**
Articulated trucks **16-17**
Box body truck **14-15**
Cars **2-13**
Car controls **4-5**
Convertibles **2-3**
Curtain-sider truck **14**
Dragsters **8-9**
Drop-sider truck **14-15**
Emergency vehicles **12-13**
Estate cars **2-3**
Fire engines **12-13**
Flatbed body truck **14-15**
Formula One cars **7**
Hatchbacks **2-3**

Hot rods **8**
Milk tanker **21**
Off-road vehicles **10-11**
Petrol tanker **20**
Police cars **12-13**
Racing cars **7, 8-9**
Rally cars **9**
Refuse truck **23**
Road sweeper **22**
Saloon cars **23**
Snow plough **22**
Sports cars **6-7**
Tankers **20-21**
Trucks **14-23**
Ultra-heavy hauler **23**

Edited by Nicola Wright & Dee Turner
Series concept Tony Potter
Design Manager Kate Buxton
Printed in China

ISBN 1 84138 655 3

10 9 8 7 6 5 4 3 2 1

This edition first published in 2003 by
Chrysalis Children's Books
The Chrysalis Building, Bramley Rd, London W10 6SP

Copyright © Chrysalis Books PLC